A few days in Krakow

Adam Kisiel, Agnieszka Kisiel

Krakow, 2012. Second edition 2020.

ISBN 9798613001804

2020 Update

Dear travelers,

it has been eight years since we published the first version of our guide "A few days in Krakow", and although what we recommend to see did not change, we decided that our guide needs important updates in two areas: best restaurants and best places to stay, as both the restaurant scene and accommodation options in Krakow have significantly evolved since 2012.

Here is what you need to know.

In the last eight years Krakow has seen an enormous growth of tourist traffic. Many new restaurants have opened (Krakow is now thought to be one of best European cities in terms of the culinary scene) and the number of new hotels, and, most importantly, apartments for rent has also grown. The most important change that we would like to emphasize is that we no longer recommend hotels as the best place to stay during your trip to Krakow. There is now a vast choice of apartments for rent available via websites such as Airbnb and Booking, and we feel that it is truly an optimal choice for anybody who would like to spend a wonderful few days in Krakow. The apartments are usually considerably cheaper and offer a high standard of accommodation, often much better than hotels, while making it easier to avoid tourist crowds. To make sure that the apartment meets your standards and needs, we highly recommend staying in an apartment managed by a renowned company, not a private owner – this guarantees the comfort and privacy of your own place, combined with service and cleanliness matching or exceeding the standard found in the best hotels.

Since the choice of apartments for rent in Krakow is huge, we would like to recommend three of them that we believe are a great choice.

Best apartment to stay for a romantic weekend for couples

If you'd like to spend a romantic time in Krakow with your partner, we recommend "Classy & Romantic apartment on Ujejskiego street" (https://www.airbnb.com/rooms/36870926).

This wonderful studio is located in very quiet district, called Salwator, that allows you to go everywhere on foot, but offers unmatched privacy and access to green areas in Krakow (Blonia Meadows, Planty park and many others).

Best apartment to stay for unmatched location and apartment design

If you'd like to feel like you are in the very center of everything, and you'd like your apartment to have a more industrial design, we recommend the "Star Design & View Apartment on Piwna street" (https://www.airbnb.com/rooms/19580562).

This one bedroom apartment is located on Piwna street – on the riverbanks of the Vistula river, right next to the famous "Love Bridge" that connects two historical districts, Podgorze and Kazimierz. The location allows you to go everywhere on foot, and some of the best restaurants in town are one minute walk from it. The simple, industrial design of the apartment has been praised by both guests and designers.

Best apartment to stay if you'd like to feel that you have your own home in Krakow

If privacy and peace are your priorities, and you'd like to feel like you have your own modern home in Krakow, we recommend the "Quiet & Private Two Room Apartment with Balcony on Slomnicka street" (https://www.airbnb.com/rooms/39361164).

This apartment is wonderfully located in a quiet Slomnicka street, that allows you to go everywhere on foot but is a guarantee of peace and being away from tourist crowds. The design of the apartment makes guests feel cosy, comfortable and like at home. The apartment is close to a great food market, where you can do your shopping while in Krakow.

Best restaurants in Krakow

This is also an area that has changed significantly since 2012. Firstly, the restaurants Ancora and Aperitif that we recommended are sadly no longer open. Secondly, so many new restaurants have opened since the last edition of our guide book that we feel that we need to update the list and recommend these places:

Best restaurants with traditional Polish cuisine

Best restaurants with traditional Polish cuisine, yet served in a modern and creative way, are Pod Nosem Restaurant and Art Restaurant, both located on the oldest street in Krakow, Kanonicza street.

A restaurant that offers the best value for money

A restaurant that offers the best value for money is undoubtedly the French Zazie Bistro, located on Jozefa street in the district of Kazimierz. A winner of the prestigious Bib Gourmand Michelin award, Zazie bistro offers great price to quality ratio and a great experience overall.

Best unconventional restaurant in Krakow

Last but not least – there is a restaurant in Krakow, that allows you to eat some of the most surprising (and delicious) dishes that you might not even have heard of. Karakter, which you can find on Brzozowa street specializes in giblets. Ostrich stomach, colt thymus, beef midriff – give it a try.

We are happy to say that nothing else changed – Krakow is still a wonderful, inexpensive, safe city that has more to offer than you think. Come to visit it any time (it looks wonderful also in winter), and, most importantly, have fun!

The authors

CONTENTS:

From the authors

A few words about Krakow

Transportation

    Balice Airport

    Getting from the airport to the center

    The Krakow Central station (trains and buses)

    Coming to Krakow in your own car

The essential things to know

    Tourist information centers

    Standard price ranges

    Money exchange and paying with credit cards

    Language and communication

    Souvenirs and what to bring as a present from Poland

    Safety

    Cabs

What to see in Krakow

    The Old Town and Main Square

    The underground of Main Square

    Sukiennice - The Clothes Hall

    Barbakan

    St Florian's Gate

    St. Mary's Basilica

    Jagiellonian University Collegium Maius

    Wawel Castle and cathedral

    Planty

    Jewish district Kazimierz, Szeroka street, Plac nowy square

    Old synagogue

    The Remuh Synagogue

    Remuh Cemetery

    Wolf Popper Synagogue

    Nowa Huta, communist-era district

- Błonia Park, big meadow close to the historical center
- Wieliczka Salt Mine

Museums, exhibitions and cultural establishments

- Czartoryski Museum and the "Lady with an Ermine"
- Archeological Museum
- National Museum
- Juliusz Słowacki theatre
- Galicia Jewish Museum
- Polish Aviation Museum
- Łaźnia Nowa theatre
- Museum of Contemporary Art

Free festivals and cyclical events

- Students festival Wianki
- The Soup Festival
- The annual Royal Dachshund Parade
- New Year's Eve
- Jewish Culture Festival

Best places to stay

- Three best hostels
- Three best reasonably priced hotels
- Three best luxury hotels

Restaurants

- Fine dining
- Reasonably priced
- Quick snack

Three things to try

- Pierogi (dumplings)
- Piołunówka (wormwood vodka)
- Polish beers and vodkas

Most popular pubs and clubs

Places connected to the famous Krakow inhabitants

- "The Papal window"
- Wisława Szymborska grave, Rakowicki cemetery,

Piotr Skrzynecki monument

Czesław Milosz grave

Krakow symbols

The Wawel Dragon

Horse-drawn carriages

Krakow pretzel

Map of Krakow center

The Wawel Cathedral

From the authors

Dear readers,

We are proud to present you with this short travel guide to Poland's most beautiful city, Krakow. It is a city we live in, know and love, and we hope to at least show you why, if not to make you feel the same.

Our guide is certainly not meant to be a comprehensive historical chronicle of the city and its monuments, as that would require something akin to an encyclopedia. In fact, we've seen many tourist guides that drown their readers in facts and factoids, the luckless visitor ambling along the streets with their nose in a thick book and never actually seeing the sights they are reading about. Moreover, with information being so easily available nowadays, we have decided that a modern guide must, first and foremost, be handy.

The city of Krakow is very open towards visitors from all countries, and in-depth information about every worthwhile object and place is available right there, so our guide simply outlines the best sightseeing possibilities for a few days in Krakow. Should you require more historical details, you can read about them on site. However, you will not find information on actual hostel and hotel quality, restaurants, cab-related pitfalls or price ranges in a Tourist Information point, and these, among others, are what we've giving you now.

We've said a lot about what we do not want this guide to be. What we do want, is to make your stay in Krakow as pleasurable and uncomplicated as possible, and our guide can make it so - with the additional advantage of not forcing you to lug a clumsy book around.

A few words about Krakow

Krakow (also Cracow or Kraków) is one of the oldest cities in Poland, and also the second largest with the population of approximately 800,000 inhabitants. The city is a traditional tourist destination due to its immense cultural, sightseeing and leisure possibilities. Sometimes referred to as the "south capital of Poland", (it was Poland's capital from 1038 to 1596), Krakow is a very old city that has retained a large portion of its medieval feel intact. It is, among others, known for having the largest medieval town square in Europe.

Sculptures and the baroque facade of the Saints Peter and Paul Church

Today, Krakow has established its popularity as Poland's largest academic and artistic centre. The Old Town attracts countless visitors with over six thousand historic sites and countless works of art. Krakow is also famous for its night-life : the myriad of hotels and hostels, restaurants, pubs, coffee houses, bars and clubs guarantee that the party never stops.

So, if you are in Poland and would like to spend a few days in Krakow, this brief guide, written by two locals, will provide you with all the information you need to make your time here as enjoyable and worthwhile as possible, regardless of your budget and goals.

Transportation

Balice Airport
Medweckiego 1 street

John Paul II International Airport Krakow-Balice is an international airport located in a village of Balice, approximately 10 km (7 miles) west of Krakow. It is open to all main international standard and low-cost carriers. There is a website where you can check available carriers and flights: http://krakowairport.pl/en

Getting from the airport to the center

The fastest and easiest way is to take the "Balice express" train, which is intended exclusively to take passengers directly to the Krakow center. It runs every day of the week from 4.30 a.m. to 11 p.m. in regular intervals of 30 minutes. The ticket costs 10 PLN (about 3 $ / 2,5 €), is available to buy directly on the train and the fee includes luggage transportation regardless of its size and weight. The train also brings you right to The Krakow Central railway station, which is directly adjacent to the Old Town (5 min. on foot).

The Krakow Central station (trains and buses)
Jan Nowak – Jeziorański square 1

The Krakow Central station is located in a large nineteenth century building, interesting in its own right. Trains from all national destinations arrive here, as well as internationals such as Berlin and Hamburg (Germany), Budapest (Hungary), Bucharest (Romania), Kiev, Lviv and Odessa (Ukraine), Prague (Czech Republic) and Vienna (Austria). The station is directly connected to a big shopping mall, Galeria Krakowska, where you will find all the necessary commodities including ATMs, pharmacies, restaurants and groceries.

Should you come to Krakow by bus, the main bus station is a part of The Krakow Central station, and all national and international buses also arrive here.

Coming to Krakow in your own car

If you plan to come to Krakow by your own car, the main issue you encounter will be where to leave it, because similar to Rome, the city center is completely closed to car traffic.

There are two chief solutions. You can stay at a hotel which has got its own parking lot (like the Sheraton or Radisson, see 'Hotels' section for more info), and the problem is solved. Or, if you prefer to stay at one of the numerous hostels, or a smaller hotel without its own garage, there is an underground parking lot in the city center, in direct neighborhood of Wawel Castle (Na Groblach square 24). It is open to the public for a fee : one day's stay is about 60 PLN (20 $ / 15 €). You can make a reservation online at http://www.parkingpodziemnykrakow.pl/en/index.html

The essential things to know

Tourist information centers

Krakow is a city that really reaches out to its visitors. One of the signs of that are the Tourist Information Points, where a friendly English-speaking staff will help you with all kind of enquiries and provide with town maps and information. You can get a free Krakow map in foreign languages there, which is highly recommended due to the city's medieval nature. The Tourist Information Points are open from 9 a.m till 7.p.m (June to October), and from 9 a.m till 5 p.m. (November to May.)

Here is a list of Tourist Information Points in Krakow :

Wszystkich Świętych Square 2

phone : 12 616 18 86

simwyspianski@infokrakow.pl

Św. Jana street 2

phone : 12 421 77 87

simjan@infokrakow.pl

Balice Airport

phone : 12 285 53 41

simbalice@infokrakow.pl

Szpitalna street 25

phone : 12 432 01 10

simszpitalna@infokrakow.pl

Józefa street 7

phone : 12 422 04 71

simjozef@infokrakow.pl

Powiśle street 11

phone : 513 099 688

simpowisle@infokrakow.pl

Sukiennice (Cloth Hall, the building In the center of the Main Square)

Main Square 1-3

phone : 12 433 73 10

sukiennice@infokrakow.pl

Standard price ranges

Krakow is not a very expensive city by European standards. Of course, there are some really expensive hotels and restaurants, but they are by no means your only choice ; reasonably priced places that still offer a good quality service can be easily found more or less everywhere, since the city is oriented towards tourists and students.

Here is a handy list of exemplary prices - the neighborhood of these figures is what you should expect:

Cab ride 10 km / 7 miles – 25 PLN / 8 $ / 6 €

A large beer (half a liter, a little less than a pint) – 8 PLN / 2,5 $ / 2 €

Lunch for one person in an averagely priced restaurant – 50 PLN / 15 $ / 12 €

Bottle of wine in an averagely priced restaurant - 50 PLN / 15 $ / 12 €

Lunch for one person in a more costly restaurant – 150 PLN / 45 $ / 36 €

Bottle of wine in a more costly restaurant - 100 PLN / 30 $ / 24 €

A hot sandwich in a fast food bar – 12 PLN / 4 $ / 3 €

An average museum ticket – 20 PLN / 7 $ / 5 €

Money exchange and paying with credit cards

The most important thing you have to remember - or, more precisely, avoid - is exchanging your money in the offices placed directly on the airports, train stations, and in the city proper - on the Main Square and Floriańska street.
Exchange offices placed there are universally known to have the least profitable rates. You will get much better rates if you will take a few minutes walk to one of the less obvious points, like on the Sławkowska or Karmelicka street - they are easy to find and the several meters distance makes a significant difference.

Of course, it is nowadays possible to use a foreign credit and debit cards almost everywhere, and the lowest acceptable payment amount is usually 10 PLN (3,5 $ / 2,5 €), which is a rather small sum. It is hence very common for the visitors to not exchange their money at all. But if you want to broaden your horizons and really feel you're abroad - not so easy nowadays that Europe has a common currency - just remember not to use the "obvious" exchange points.

Language and communication

Polish language is traditionally regarded as one of the most difficult European languages and nigh-impossible for foreigners to learn (according to their own words). Fortunately, in modern Poland the command of English language is ranked among the most important skills and English is widely taught in majority of public and private schools, so it is likely that an average person on the street will understand the basics.

That is what most of the country is like, at any rate. Krakow, being a cosmopolitan city with a rather multi-cultural population, its orientation towards tourism and education, is one of our cities that have the highest percentage of English-speaking inhabitants. While hiring the staff for hotels, restaurants and cultural establishments, the candidates' command of English is always an essential condition. Nearly all restaurant menus, hotel signs and cultural leaflets are bilingual by default, so you can easily assume that communication will surely not be a problem.

Souvenirs and what to bring as a present from Poland

The Sukiennice (the large, mainly-Renaissance building in the middle of the Main Square), a historical market trade center is where you can find a big selection of stands with Polish souvenirs nowadays. Traditionally the most popular gifts from Poland include:

Facade of the Clothes Hall (Sukiennice)

- Amber jewelry, decorations or figurines (the history of our amber trade reaches as far back as the 1st century A.D.)
- Original and untypical alcoholic beverages, like meads (honey-based alcohols), natural cordials, especially those brewed by one of Krakow's monasteries, and of course world-famous polish vodka. The best vodka brands are Wyborowa, Żubrówka or Belweder (known abroad as Belvedere).
- Regional candy and delicacies - boiled mallow sweets, natural jams and honey (Polish honey is highly regarded by chefs around the world) or smoked cold meats are good choices for cooking enthusiasts.
- Items connected with the Jewish culture, like Kippah, which can be bought in Kazimierz.

Traditional vodka shop

Safety

The alarm phone number is the same as for all European countries – 112. There are numerous police stations in the city : two placed conveniently in the center proper - one directly on the Main Square (Main Square 27), and the second in the Jewish district Kazimierz (Szeroka street 35). There is always an English-speaking officer on duty, so in the case of any trouble, do not hesitate to visit the police station - they are well accustomed to the mishaps and difficulties a visitor might face.

Krakow is a large and bustling city, and no different than others in that regard. However, the streets are usually packed with people and the old town - which has, admittedly, some narrow, dark alleys - is crowded more or less at all hours and frequently patrolled by the municipal police. All in all, the city is very safe for such a cosmopolitan place, and reasonably prudent visitors should mostly worry about their pockets being picked.

Just to be on the safe side, it is a very good idea to add an ICE number to your mobile phone contact book. ICE is an "In case of emergency" number, and it means a person who can provide the emergency personnel, such as the police or paramedics, with necessary information. Simply put a number of such a person - a family member, a close friend - into your contact book and name it "ICE". It may save you a lot of trouble.

Cabs

The historical centre of the city is closed to car traffic - a practice common in Europe nowadays. For this reason, sightseeing in Krakow is usually done on foot. Nevertheless, there will certainly occur an occasion when you need a cab.
What you should be aware of in that case? There are numerous cab companies operating in the city, but the laws also allow for private carriers, who unfortunately try to disguise themselves as ordinary cabs. They usually charge much higher fees, sometimes going as far as ten times the cost of a normal cab. When in doubt, ask the driver for an estimate cost to your destination beforehand. Legitimate cab drivers will have no problem with this and will gladly tell you the approximate total up front.

What to see in Krakow

The Old Town and Main Square

Krakow Old Town is the most impressive asset of the city. It is featured on the UNESCO World Heritage List and attracts many visitors and tourists from all over the world. Unlike Poland's current capital, Warsaw, it has survived the World War II untouched and has not changed much since the thirteenth century.

The Main Square (Rynek Glowny) is the biggest medieval town square in Europe. It is the heart of the city, and a place where social life never stops. Main Square is surrounded by a ring of townhouses - a practice common in the Middle Ages and kept up in the following centuries. These townhouses present a variety of styles, ranging from the 14th century onwards, and each has its own historical significance.

The whole Main Square and Old Town holds numerous historical monuments. The most important and impressive of them will be described in the subsequent sections.

The underground of Main Square

Archeological research had recently shown that the Krakow Main Square as it is now was actually superimposed over an even older marketplace structure, fragments of which can even be dated back to the eleventh century. In 2010, an underground museum has been opened directly under the Main Square to make these findings available to the public. It covers over a six thousands square meters, and the underground exhibition showcases the history of Krakow that spans over a millennium, mixing archeological exhibits, fastidious reconstruction and modern technology to make the experience as accessible and enjoyable as possible.

Main Square Underground is hugely popular, and getting a ticket without a reservation usually requires hours of waiting. You can save time and ensure you will get in by making an online reservation at http://www.bilety.podziemiarynku.com/

Sukiennice - The Clothes Hall

The large, Renaissance building right in the middle of the Main Square is often mistaken for a city hall. What it actually is, however, is a medieval analogy to today's shopping mall: a place where merchants could rent stall space and sell their products. Such an object existed in this exact part of Krakow as far back as the 13th century, although it was quite different then what is there nowadays. The building that stands on the square now has been built in 1556-1559, and the impressive still structure dares you not to notice it.

In the past, only the richest merchants could afford a stall in the Cloth Hall and they mostly offered expensive fabrics and overseas goods such as spice. Currently, Sukiennice houses exhibitions, but in keeping up with tradition, the walk-through hall is packed with souvenir stands.

Barbakan

If you arrive at the main train station or the bus station, you will certainly pass the Barbakan when going to the Old Town. Barbakan - The Krakow Barbican – is a small fortress just outside the city walls. Like the St Florian's Gate, Barbakan is a vestige of the medieval fortification system. In its days of glory, it was occupied by armed soldiers who have been checking everybody approaching Krakow city walls. It is possible to visit the interior of the Barbakan itself, and if you are lucky, you can also attend the demonstration of medieval swordfighting, regularly shown there.

St Florian's Gate

St Florian's Gate is a Gothic tower, kept in great condition and once an important element of the city's 14th century defense system. Very close to another element of the bailey, Barbakan, St Florian's Gate is one of the symbols of Krakow and an unofficial "Main entrance" to the Old Town. It is also the beginning of the Royal Route, a traditional route for parades, important foreign visitors, and, most importantly, the historical coronation processions. Today, St Florian's Gate is typically the first place visitors begin their sightseeing at and a place where many street artists and musicians present their works.

St. Mary's Basilica

This brick Gothic church, built in the 13th century, is undoubtedly one of the most recognizable symbols of the city and a prominent fixture of the Main Square. Inside you will find the famous wooden altarpiece - the largest Gothic altar in the world - made by Veit Stoss in the 15th century. The intricate woodwork and astonishingly detailed, anatomically correct statues took the master sculptor 12 years to complete.

Sideview of the Basilica

Every full hour a signal, played on the trumpet, can be heard on the Main Square. The trumpeter plays it on the very top of the Basilica tower, repeating it four times in all directions, and each time the melody is cut short before the finish. Legend has it that the trumpeter, at one time in the 13th century, has played the signal to warn the city of Tatar riders (it was the period of the Mongol invasion). The forewarned citizens managed to shut the gates in time, but a Tatar archer had shot the trumpeter and thus the signal was cut short. Though the legend itself is probably a modern invention, the signal is played in that fashion every hour.

Today, you can visit the Basilica interior, admire the altarpiece, and then climb the tower to see the trumpeter's window and a beautiful view of the Old Town.

Jagiellonian University Collegium Maius
Jagiellońska 15 street

The *Collegium Maius* is the oldest building belonging to the Jagiellonian University, the oldest and most respected university in Krakow and the entire country. Jagiellonian University is also the second oldest university in Eastern Europe (the oldest is in Prague, Czech Republic) and one of the oldest universities in the world. Founded in the middle of 14th century, it has been the place of education of such famous scholars as Nicolaus Copernicus – world famous astronomer, Jan Dlugosz - a historian, Jan Kochanowski – a famous polish poet, or, later, Pope John Paul II.

While Jagiellonian University is still a very active and currently also a very modern educational institution, inside the Collegium Maius you will be able to feel the atmosphere as it was in the times of the medieval scholars, reading their manuscripts in silence and concentration.

Wawel Castle and cathedral

The Kings' Castle on Wawel hill is an enormous, impressive castle structure which has its beginnings in the ninth century. The castle proper is surrounded by other buildings, including the Wawel Cathedral - the historical chapel of Poland's Queens and Kings. It is directly adjacent to the center of the Old Town and borders upon the Vistula River. It is a very important place to the history of Poland, the traditional royal residence when Krakow was our capital and the place where nearly all the Polish rulers have been crowned. The Wawel Cathedral is still a place of enormous national significance today - the tombs of the old kings still rest there, and to be buried on Wawel is the biggest honor and has happened only once in the modern history of Poland. Among its many exhibits it houses the "Szczerbiec" - "The Notched Sword" - the coronation sword of the Polish monarchs.

The Wawel Cathedral

The entire complex is maintained in perfect condition, and organized in a way that allows for the full enjoyment of its architecture and history for visitors from all over the world. Nearly all museums and exhibitions there offer an assistance of an English-speaking guide, or the automated recordings with commentary in various foreign languages, which ensures you will always know what are you looking at and make visiting Wawel an enjoyable and memorable experience.

The other side of Wawel

TIP: The best time to visit Wawel Castle is the morning on a working day - the afternoons and weekends attract huge crowds.

Planty

Planty is an old walk-park in a very interesting round shape. It circles the whole Old Town, the ring shape being a vestige of the medieval city walls - a testimony of the walls' course and the city's old borders. Nowadays, it is an oasis of peace and quiet, offering contact with nature in the middle of the city. It is one of the biggest parks in Krakow, with its circumference reaching 4 kilometers (2.5 miles) and filled with ancient, huge trees that fit right with the city's history. By walking through Planty you can easily reach most of the notable monuments based in the Old Town. You can also reach Wawel Castle and the shore of the Vistula river easily. Because of that, many Krakow inhabitants often choose to take a refreshing - if, admittedly, slightly longer - route by Planty rather than the shorter way through city streets in their everyday business.

TIP: Spend some time simply sitting on a bench and taking in the slow, friendly atmosphere of the city, which is especially apparent on Planty.

Jewish district Kazimierz, Szeroka street, Plac nowy square

Jewish merchants' shingles

Kazimierz is a historical Jewish district of Krakow. In modern history, it has gained a significant notoriety because after the deplorable dwindling of the Jewish population due to World War II, it has been a cheap-rent district with a large crime rate. This negative tendency is fortunately in the course of changing, though, mainly because of the annual Festival of the Jewish Culture held in the summer. In 1993 Kazimierz was chosen as a set for the famous Steven Spielberg movie, *The Schindler's List*, which has drawn more visitors to the district and encouraged its renovation. Currently Kazimierz is nearly completely renovated, and can present its historical monuments proudly. It is also a fashionable district full of restaurants, bars and pubs.

Szeroka street

Szeroka street ("Szeroka" meaning "Wide") is, alongside the Plac Nowy square, the heart of Kazimierz. It is where the Festival of Jewish Culture takes place, and where you will find the most important Jewish historic monuments: The Old Synagogue (Szeroka street 24), The Remuh Synagogue (Szeroka street 40), Remuh Cemetery (Szeroka street 40) and the Wolf Popper Synagogue (Szeroka street 16).

Restaurants on each side of Wolf Popper Synagogue

Plac Nowy square (The New Square), also known as the "Jewish" square, is the second biggest public place in Kazimierz. It holds some events of the Jewish Cultural Festival, and many other events, like the annual Soup Festival. In the center of the Plac Nowy square you will find a characteristic round building, rather like a large market stall, which offers many quick snacks, including zapiekanka, a long, roasted or grilled sandwich with mushrooms, ham, molten cheese and many other ingredients which is the most popular street-food in Poland, easily beating hot-dogs, hamburgers and other Western imports.

Plac nowy square

TIP: If you decide on trying zapiekanka, choose the window with the sign which says "U Endziora" (At Endzior's). These guys are masters.

TIP 2: Be sure to try at least one traditional Jewish dish. You will be positively surprised.

Old synagogue
Szeroka 24 street

Old synagogue is the oldest and biggest synagogue in Krakow, placed in the Jewish district Kazimierz and dated back to 15th century (the structure itself had been rebuilt in Renaissance style around 1570). The Jewish district has been devastated by the Nazis during the World War II, and the synagogue itself had been used as a magazine, obliterating the rich religious, cultural and social life it housed before. Fortunately it has been subsequently renovated and transformed into a museum exhibiting a rich collection of art depicting the Jewish society in Poland throughout the ages, as well as elements of traditional Jewish clothing or sacral paraphernalia. The building itself remains one of the best examples of Jewish sacral architecture in the whole of Europe, and one of the most important places for the followers of Judaism.

The Remuh Synagogue

Szeroka 40 street

The Remuh Synagogue was built in 1553, and tradition ascribes its foundation to Israel ben Josef, who wanted to honour his wife Malka, killed by an epidemic. It is smaller than the Old Synagogue, but is worth visiting because it is the only synagogue which still performs regular religious services. It is also well-known for its interior, the courtyard walls inscribed with the names of those who died in the Holocaust and an ornamental bimah, a special elevated platform for reading Torah aloud.

Remuh Cemetery
Szeroka 40 street

Also known as "the old cemetery of Krakow", the small Remuh cemetery is an ancient graveyard, founded in 1535. Located next to the Remuh Synagogue, the cemetery actually predates the temple. Although it had shared the fate of all Judaic structures during the World War II, it has been renovated and is now an enclave of peace and contemplation in the very middle of the city. Many notable figures from the Jewish community are buried there, including Rabbi Mosses Isserles, famous for his Ashkenazi-oriented commentaries to the Jewish traditions.

Wolf Popper Synagogue
Szeroka 16 street

Named after its founder, the wealthy merchant Wolf Popper, this small synagogue had been built in 1620 and equipped most sumptuously - historical records claim that the temple's opulent furnishings were so expensive in maintenance that it brought Wolf Popper's descendants to the brink of bankruptcy. Of course, all objects of value have been robbed by the Nazis and only written accounts remain. The synagogue operates currently as a Youth Cultural Centre, with an emphasis on the Jewish cultural tradition, but the inside is of course open to tourists and the admission is free.

Nowa Huta, communist-era district

Nowa Huta ("The new steel mill") is a huge district of Krakow, placed away from the city center. It has been artificially planned as a completely new town near Krakow by the communist government in the early nineteen-fifties, the first buildings actually erected in 1949. The idea was to counterweight the artistic and intellectual atmosphere of Krakow - which was seen as suspect by the communist regime - by the more "appropriate" laborer inhabitants of Nowa Huta, and the actual steel mill was built to offer them employment.

Sign of the historical steel mill

Today, Nowa Huta is certainly worth visiting for its socialist-realism buildings and Tadeusz Sendzimir Mill (place of very important labor strikes during the 80s). It also begins to revive its cultural life nowadays : the very modern, buoyant theatre Łaźnia Nowa (Osiedle Szkolne 25 street) is especially worth mentioning. It presents many critically-acclaimed contemporary plays (with English subtitles presented on special screens).

TIP: because of the communist legacy of Nowa Huta, there are many organized tours, which aim to provide visitors with the ultimate socialist tourism experience : for one day you are driven around in an old communist car - the "Trabant" - you admire the post-communist buildings, you eat the dreadful and very cheap food in a gloomy, dirty diner and finally you visit a small musty apartment, where you drink warm vodka with a 70-year old who remembers when the first brick has been laid there in Nowa Huta. If you are a fan of original experiences, it is definitely worth trying. Currently the best guide company specializing in this kind of trips is "Crazy Guides", and you can book such a trip online at http://www.crazyguides.com/

A Trabant car

TIP 2: If you decide to take a guided Nowa Huta tour, do not avoid drinking alcohol. Post-communist district goes really well with a few shots of vodka and can actually be rather downbeat when viewed sober.

Błonia Park, big meadow close to the historical center

Błonia is the largest green spot in Krakow, a very large meadow which lies very close to the center of the city. It is commonly visited for sports, all sorts of physical recreation and outdoor leisure. It is worth visiting because, one, you can just lie around there and relax, and two, you do not see a huge grassland directly in the heart of the big city every day. Unless you live in Krakow, of course. Błonia have been a place of many important historical events, including enormous Masses celebrated by Pope John Paul II.

TIP: Visit Błonia only if you are visiting Krakow in the spring or summer. In the colder seasons it is naturally quite deserted and doesn't offer much.

Wieliczka Salt Mine
Jan Mikołaj Daniłowicz 25 street, Wieliczka

In the small town of Wieliczka (about 10 kilometers / 7 miles from Krakow) lies a salt mine, which has been in use since 13th century and which may be one of the most impressive things you will ever see in your life. The salt mine, which has been an important source of revenue to the city of Krakow for centuries, was ran by the same mercantile company since its inception, and that company is now listed among the oldest in the world. Tourist attractions include a walk through the mine's tunnels and caves, with statues sculpted in salt blocks and an entire chapel (Chapel of St Kinga) carved out of salt - the walls, the floor, the stairs, the altar. There even is an underground lake in the mine and some trips include swimming on it in a canoe.

It is a hugely popular and memorable spot, with over 1 million visitors every year. It is a place worth visiting by any means, and the best way to go about it is to make an online reservation at https://www.ebilety.kopalnia.pl (English version of the site available). Apart from the "regular" visiting tours, the mine hosts concerts, theatre plays and opera performances, information on which can be found on the site.

TIP: Be sure to book a ticket which includes swimming in the underground lake. It is twice as awesome as it sounds.

Museums, exhibitions and cultural establishments

Krakow has always been the cultural center of Poland, and is often related to as "the cultural capital of Poland". Cultural life in XXI century is as vivid and animated as ever. If you will have some ample time, it is certainly worth to visit the most important Krakow museums and exhibitions.

Czartoryski Museum and the "Lady with an Ermine"
Św. Jana 19 street

Czartoryski Museum is the most notable museum in Krakow, founded by Princess Izabela Czartoryska in 1796. Well – preserved and located in the very middle of the city, Czartoryski Museum is in the possession of many invaluable works of art, gathered over the centuries by the aristocratic, immensely wealthy Czartoryski family who were renowned as art collectors. Perhaps the most famous and valuable artifact you can see there is the "Lady with an Ermine", the famous Leonardo da Vinci painting from the end of the 15th century.

TIP: This priceless work of art is a great reason alone to visit the Czartoryski Museum, however, if it is not enough for you, among many other fascinating showpieces is an entire exhibition of ancient Egyptian artifacts. You will see the mysterious mummies (including an actual mummy of a cat), ancient talismans, and will hear strange noises from behind the shadowy sarcophagi.

Archeological Museum
Senacka 3 street

It is the oldest archeological Museum in Poland, established in 1850. It is located in an old palace, which has been connected to the system of medieval city walls. The building is surrounded by a beautiful garden, which can be visited independently. The museum hosts many exhibitions, including the complete archeological history of southeastern Poland. There are also exhibitions which do not concern Polish history, like the ancient Egypt exhibition (called "The Gods of Ancient Egypt").

National Museum
3 maja 1 avenue

This impressive, monumental building, situated by the Blonia park, is the biggest department of the Polish National Museum (which has many smaller branches, such as the Czartoryski Museum). It holds interesting permanent exhibitions, such as the "Gallery of the Twentieth Century Polish Art", with the paintings of famous polish painters (W.Tetmajer, J.Malczewski and many others). It also holds many temporary exhibitions, so there is a chance you will see something new every time you go there. In 2011, for example, the biggest success of the National Museum was the exhibition called "The Painter of Elements", showing the paintings of great British artist William Turner.

TIP: The museum is traditionally closed on Mondays, so pick another day to visit.

Juliusz Słowacki theatre
Świętego Ducha 1 square

If you go on foot from the main train station to the Old Town (it is very likely you will do so), on you will notice a huge, very impressive baroque building on your left. It is the Juliusz Slowacki theatre, named by one of the most important Polish poets from the 19th century, author of many symbolic dramas relating to the important factors of Polish national conscience.

The huge theatre was the place of many important cultural events of historical significance, and made admiring great Polish actors possible. Today, it is still vibrantly active, and tries to reconcile its traditional approach with a modern opinions on theatre. The building is famous for its luxury interiors, and its boxes will make you feel like the Phantom of the Opera is about to jump out at you any moment now.

Galicia Jewish Museum
Dajwór 18 street

Entirely concentrated on Jewish culture and history, Galicia Jewish Museum hosts many interesting exhibitions and events, including "Traces of the Memory", photographic exhibition of eight hundred years of Jewish presence in southeastern Poland. The museum also organizes regular concerts of traditional klezmer music.

Polish Aviation Museum
Jan Paweł II 39 avenue

Polish Aviation Museum is an immensely popular exhibition of Polish aviation history, with a huge outdoor area where vintage aircrafts are shown. Located on an old, unused airport, museum presents over 215 aircrafts including some models used by the famous No. 303 Polish Fighter Squadron, a renown pilot squad which served in the Royal Air Force during the World War II.

You can see a detailed gallery of the museum at www.muzeumlotnictwa.pl/

TIP: Because a big part of the museum is located outdoors, it is the best to enjoy this establishment in the late spring or summer.

Łaźnia Nowa theatre
Os. Szkolne 25 street

This is the youngest theatre in Krakow (established in 2005). Located in the post-industrial buildings in post-communist district Nowa Huta, Łaźnia Nowa (meaning "A new bath house") has quickly achieved the reputation of a dynamic and modern cultural establishment, with many important premieres and shows. It is a very friendly place for foreign visitors, with most of its plays shown with English subtitles on special screens.

Museum of Contemporary Art
Lipowa 4 street

Again, it is the youngest museum in Krakow (established in 2010) but it has already managed to achieve the status of an important place on a cultural map of the city. It is situated in the old halls of Schindler's factory, using its vast spaces to present contemporary art of the last two decades. The museum also runs many educational and cultural activities, as well as the multilingual bookstore, library and the sound, visual and design galleries.

Free festivals and cyclical events

Students festival Wianki

When: June, usually during the summer solstice or near the date

Where: near the Wawel Castle, on the bank of Vistula river

Wianki (meaning "the flower chaplets", and named after an old Slavic Pagan tradition of throwing flower wreaths onto a river on Midsummer Night) is an annual outdoor festival, located on the bank of the river Vistula, near the Wawel Castle. It is a massive event, attended by students and youths en masse, but completely free and open to people of all ages and cultures. It has evolved from a traditional summer solstice outdoor event to a free for all music festival, often honored by famous international stars like Marillion, Lenny Kravitz or Jamiroquai.

The Soup Festival

When: in the end of may

Where: Plac Nowy square, Jewish district Kazimierz

This event is much smaller than the attended-by-thousands Wianki, but it may be easily called a most friendly, homy and cosy Krakow festival. During one day in May, all the restaurants and pubs prepare their own unique soup, which they distribute for free to everybody who attends the festival. Accompanied by live music on the Plac Nowy square, the soups compete for the title of the Year's best soup.

The annual Royal Dachshund Parade

When: September

Where: The Old Town, Main Square

A dachshund dog

Every year many proud dachshund owners choose to participate in an annual parade of these dogs from the Barbican to the Main Square. The best looking and longest dog wins the first prize. There is always a lot of jolly barking, sniffing and tail wagging - be sure to visit if you like dogs.

New Year's Eve

When: The New Year's Eve

Where: The Old Town, Main Square

Massive, free for everybody party on the New Year's Eve is one of the biggest events of this kind in Poland, usually broadcasted by TV and featuring big Polish and foreign stars. In the middle of the Main Square a huge stage is set, with concerts from the early evening till the break of dawn. When the new year begins, there is always a fireworks show, and then the party continues. Traditionally drinking outdoors is tolerated on that day, so the Polish cold winter is never an issue.

TIP: One of the favorite ways of Krakow inhabitants to celebrate this day is to gather on the main square and participate in the concerts and fireworks, and then, after midnight, go to one of the numerous clubs in the Old Town (usually on the New Year's Eve prior reservation is highly recommended).

Jewish Culture Festival

When: June/July

Where: Szeroka street, Jewish district Kazimierz

The Jewish Culture Festival has been one of the reasons that made Jewish district Kazimierz regain its popularity. The festival is a huge event, composed of concerts, plays, meetings, cultural workshops and many other attractions. The nine days long festival is usually finished by a huge final concert on the Szeroka street, with many famous klezmer musicians, but also other performers (like Frank London or Fred Wesley).

The Jewish Culture Festival is one of the most commonly known events of this type in the world, and one of the biggest and highly praised festivals in Poland. It is definitely a must-see if you plan to be in Krakow in the late June / early July.

Best places to stay

Krakow is a city which possesses one of the biggest hotel bases in Poland. You are not limited to the hotels, though. There are three main categories of accommodation : hostels, reasonably priced hotels, and luxury hotels. There are also private apartments to rent, but because it is quite hard to recommend something there and be sure that the quality of the service will remain unchanged while you, dear reader, read these words, we will not take any risk and leave the apartments outside this guide, though of course you can still book one of those with ease via the web.

Three best hostels

Mama's hostel, Bracka 4 street

www.mamashostel.com.pl

Mama's hostel is a very well-rated hostel placed directly In the Old Town. Comfy, clean, reasonably priced and close to the all tourist attractions and social life establishments, this hostel is a solid choice for your trip to Krakow.

A two-person private is 70 $ / 50 €

Flamingo hostel, Szewska 4 street

http://flamingo-hostel.com/

Again great localization, cosy rooms, helpful and friendly staff. Also, if you would like to participate in Krakow rich clublife, this hostel will be the best choice, because it is on the Szewska street, which is proud to host the most clubs in any one street in Krakow.

A two-person private is 70 $ / 50 €

Rynek 7 hostel, Main Square 7

http://www.hostelrynek7.pl/

Offering undoubtedly the best view among Krakow hostels because of its location directly on the Main Square, this hostel is a third strong choice.

A two-person private is 75 $ / 40 €

Three best reasonably priced hotels

Senacki Hotel, Grodzka 51 street

http://www.hotelsenacki.pl/

Great location and comfort for a reasonable price, especially compared to its close neighbors, like Copernicus. Placed in a fully renovated classic townhouse, offers great, cosy rooms and enjoyable atmosphere. Definitely the best choice, may even be compared to the much more expensive places, like Sheraton or Bonerowski Palace.

A two-person room is 130 $ / 100 €

Logos Hotel, Szujskiego 5 street

http://www.hotel-logos.pl/

This little gem may not be so directly in the center of the city, but is still located very nicely near Old Town. Offers really good prices without reducing the quality of your stay.

A two-person room is 110 $ / 85 €

Secesja Hotel, Paulinska street 24

http://www.hotelsecesja.pl/

A good example of a small, quiet place, with a homy atmosphere. You will find Hotel Secesja in the middle of Kazimierz, and you can still go to the Old Town by foot. Again, you will find this place reasonably priced and very comfortable.

A two-person room is 100 $ / 75 €

Three best luxury hotels

Bonerowski Palace, Main Square 42

http://www.palacbonerowski.pl/

This hotel proudly names itself "Palace" and you know what? They are right. A winner of "The best luxury hotel in Poland" award, Bonerowski Palace exceeds every needs of a visitor : elegant interiors, enormous, luxury rooms, great view onto a Main Square, placed in an UNESCO-listed edifice dating back to the Middle Ages, but with every modern commodity.

A two-person room is 650 $ / 500 €

Grand Hotel, Slawkowska 5/7 street

http://www.grand.pl

The Grand Hotel lives up to the name since 1887. Again, you will find it on the corner of the Main Square. The hotel offers comfort and privacy, great restaurant and also an impressive green terrace on the roof.

A two-person room is 325 $ / 250 €

Copernicus, Kanonicza 16 street

http://www.copernicus.hotel.com.pl

Copernicus Hotel is placed in a magical place – on the Kanonicza street, the oldest street in Krakow, which connects the Old Town to the Wawel Castle and hosts only the most respectable institutions. Copernicus prides itself with a genuine gothic façade, medieval cellars with a swimming pool, and a variety of prominent guests, including His Royal Highness Charles, Prince of Wales and U.S. president George W. Bush with his wife Laura.

A two-person room is 260 $ / 200 €

Prices for hostels and hotels are relevant for summer 2012, private rooms for hostels.

Restaurants

Fine dining

Wierzynek
Main Square 15

Probably the most famous and respected restaurant in Krakow. Founded in 1945, Wierzynek has always been a symbol of great Polish cuisine, flawless service and a place where you can really feel you are in Krakow. Located directly on the Main Square, Wierzynek prides itself with a great view on the Old Town, and historical – themed rooms: the Knights room, Pompeian rooms, and the Renaissance room. It is a great place to try the traditional dishes of Polish cuisine, like dumplings, sorrel soup, the roasted duck or the sour rabbit soup.

Ancora
Dominikańska 3 street

Praised Krakow restaurant and a finalist of many "top Polish restaurant" lists, Ancora aims to reinvent traditional Polish cuisine in a modern way, so you can expect many inventive propositions there, like blue cheese with chocolate. Very cosy and romantic, it is a great choice for spending some special time with your significant other.

Pimiento
Józefa 26 street
Stolarska 13 street

Undoubtedly the best beef steaks in Krakow. Beef is imported directly from Argentina, and offers a delightful experience to steak lovers. Apart from this, Pimiento offers great seafood, especially grilled prawns. It also handily keeps two branches : one in the Old Town, the second in the Kazimierz, so you can drop in no matter which area you are currently visiting.

Pod Aniołami
Grodzka 35 street

Another place where you will enjoy Polish cuisine served at its best. Beautiful interiors and quiet garden in a medieval courtyard make Pod Aniołami (Under Angels' Patronate) a great restaurant to try Nobleman's shashlik of pork fillet roasted in wine, grilled trout with horseradish, or even a whole baked wild boar!

Cyrano de Bergerac

Sławkowska 26 street

The best French restaurant in Krakow, named after the famous lover poet and owner of a distinct long nose. Winner of the "Best restaurant in Krakow" title (twice), Cyrano de Bergerac invites you to try some of the best specialities of French cuisine. Be sure to try Terrine of Duck Foie Gras in Cognac, Tournedos of Beef Fillet with Morel, Châteaubriand with Peppers Sauce and, above all, choose something from the impressive choice of French wines.

Reasonably priced

Starka
Józefa 14 street

Cosy and intimate place, Starka is widely considered one of the best places in the terms of quality and price. Affordable menu offers, among others, aromatic rabbit loin, tender duck or lamb in cranberry sauce. Accompanied with good selection of wines, plus a non-pretentious and friendly atmosphere, Starka guarantees a great, enjoyable experience.

Aperitif
Sienna 9 street

A very nice restaurant, located close to the Old Town. Great interiors and good view onto the "Main Square jr." a second square in the Old Town in the terms of size. Aperitif offers a good choice of tasty courses, including broiled swordfish, roast chicken or goose breast.

Three Peppers Pizzeria
Poselska 17 street

The only pizzeria on this short list, The Three Peppers is a place certainly worth visiting. Voted as "the best pizza in town" (the many Italian tourists having lunch there seem to confirm this opinion), this pizzeria serves its delicacies directly from the wood-fired oven. If you are not so into pizza, do not be alarmed – you will find also other main courses there, including a big variety of pastas and few, but very good, meats.

Corleone
Poselska 19 street

A very likeable and quiet Italian restaurant. Corleone is a bit harder to find than the other above-mentioned places (it lies in the side alley of Grodzka street), but certainly worth searching for. Try the veal escallops with shrimps and white asparagus or the great seafood mix.

Edo Sushi
Bożego Ciała 3 street

In the last few years sushi has become very popular in Krakow, resulting in many - often very expensive - sushi bars. Edo Sushi combines great quality and atmosphere (the owners are fascinated by Japanese cuisine and culture) with a great price. Sitting on the pillow at the characteristic low tables of Japan and sipping sake or delightful green tea you can enjoy the best sushi in town.

Quick snack

Moa Burger
Mikołajska 3 street

If you ever find yourself thinking about something quick to eat and eyeballing the McDonalds sign, don't go there – choose Moa Burger instead. The owner, a chef with experience gathered in New Zealand makes the best hamburgers in Krakow, composed of fresh vegetables and meats of good quality. They're not your average, dull buns either - should you go, definitely try the most impressive example – a spiced lamb with mint yoghurt hamburger!

Chimera Salad Bar
Świętej Anny 3 street

A salad bar, very popular among students. Worth visiting for its huge choice of salads (over 30 different salads) and also its original, fresh soft drinks, like the mint nectar.

Green Way
Mikołajska 14 street

A foolproof choice for vegetarians – tofu curry, cabbage and mushroom croquets, or a tasty vegetable cake (flapjack layers with spinach, leek and tomatoes). Their aloo kofta is especially good, and rosemary-seasoned dumplings appeal to Mediterranean enthusiasts. Green Way's tea and coffee are always Fair Trade, too.

Gosciniec Floriański
Floriańska 21 street

A good place to try some polish traditional dishes if you are in a hurry. Great dumplings, boletus mushroom soup or a sauerkraut stew with sausage, served in a friendly atmosphere.

Three things to try

Pierogi (dumplings)

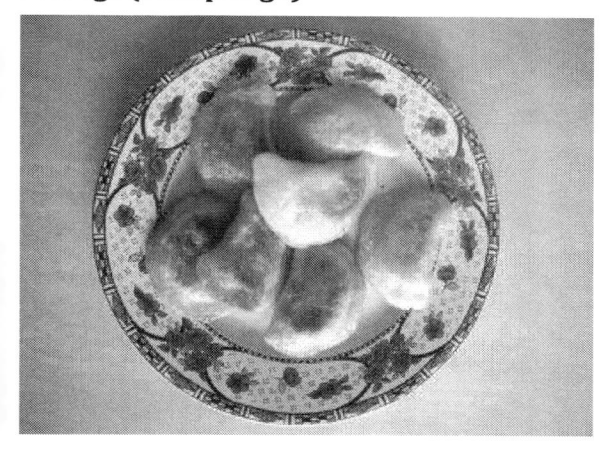

Pierogi is a traditional Slavic dish, immensely popular in Poland and one of our trademarks. Made of dough stuffed with whatever takes the cook's fancy ; the most popular fillings are meat and onion, quark cheese in different incarnations or cabbage and mushrooms, although there's practically no limit to the possibilities. Sweet fillings are also popular – fruit, fruit and cheese and similar are a staple of the summer diet. Pierogi are typically boiled and can sometimes be fried after boiling. When made right, it is a meal both delicious and satisfying, and most restaurants will offer some variant of it.

Krakow should not be visited without trying it, and a good place to do so is the restaurant "Pierożki u Vincenta", 12 Bożego Ciała Street (http://www.pierozkiuvincenta.pl)

Piołunówka (wormwood vodka)

Piołunówka is a bitter, herbal vodka, with it origins very close to the currently rare absinthe. Notorious for its alleged hallucinogenic effects (which it actually has no more than any other vodka, that is to say, it depends on how much you drink), is completely legal in Poland and very difficult to obtain anywhere else in the world. Tastes best when drank by the authors' of this book original recipe : on the rocks, with freshly squeezed lemon juice.

Polish beers and vodkas

Poland is famous for its high quality beers as well as vodkas. They are priced very reasonably, offering taste and quality, often exceeding the best foreign products in this category.

Beers to try: Żywiec, Tyskie, Lech, Brackie, Ciechan

Vodkas to try: Wyborowa, Sobieski, Żubrówka, Cherry Cordial

Most popular pubs and clubs

Pauza

Floriańska 18 street

A strong candidate to a title of "the night centre of the town", Pauza is composed of two parts: the chillout area on the first floor, and the vibrant club in the basements. There is always an art (usually photo) gallery on the first floor, as well as the famous collection of frequent visitors portraits. From Thursday till Saturday the basement club offers of high-standard parties.

Alchemia

Estery 5 street

The most popular place on Kazimierz, where you can meet everybody, from students to Polish showbusiness stars. Alchemia means an intimate atmosphere and a "feel of real Krakow". Posing mainly as a peaceful place, Alchemia (It means "The Alchemy") is also participating in the night life, hosting concerts and parties.

Dym

Tomasza 13 street

One of the most popular places in Krakow, Dym ("Smoke") is currently not drenched in smoke as it used to, since smoking is illegal in Polish pubs. However, Dym still offers artistic discussions, extensive drinking and vivid nightlife till the morning light. Fun fact: there were many attempts by other bars to compete with Dym in its closest neighborhood – without any success in the terms of popularity.

Bunkier sztuki

Szczepański 3a square

Bunkier Sztuki ("The Art Bunker") is probably a most artistic pub in Krakow, being a part of an art gallery, hosting many important exhibitions (including the annual World Press Photo gallery). Bunkier Sztuki also prides itself with the biggest summer garden in Krakow. Thanks to the unique structure, which looks very much like an old railway station, the aforementioned heated garden can be enjoyed all year.

Singer

Estery 20 street

The second night centre of Kazimierz, Singer – named after the vintage sewing machines, which currently serve as tables – is a tempting coffee house opened usually all night.

Drukarnia

Nadwislańska 1 street

A direct neighbor of Kazimierz and Vistula river, Drukarnia is a coffee house and pub in the day, a friendly club in the night.

Frantic

Szewska 5 street

Probably the most vibrant club in Krakow, frequently with a queue of would-be patrons waiting outside. Always full of beautiful women and handsome men, Frantic offers crazy, memorable parties. A lot of foreigners are usually there, so there is a big chance you will feel comfortable.

Ministerstwo

Szpitalna 1 street

Ministerstwo ("The Ministry") vibrates with the best sounds played by the best Krakow DJs: dubstep, funk, hip-hop and drum'n'bass. Big rooms and a flashy dancefloor gather a lot of Krakow vivid nightlife there.

U Louisa

Main Square 13

Again a well-known club, U Louisa is usually full of enthusiastic party-goers, enjoying live music in the renovated basements.

Kokon

Gazowa 21 street

The most important and popular gay club in Krakow. Huge dancefloor and a genuine maze of smaller rooms create a friendly space where gay clubbers of both genders can meet and party together. It's friendly towards heterosexual visitors, though the majority clientele is usually gay.

Places connected to the famous Krakow inhabitants

"The Papal window"
Franciszkańska 3 street

Pope John Paul II real name was Karol Wojtyla, and he was a Krakow bishop for many years. After he has been elected the Pope, he has been regularly visiting Krakow. During those visits, he was in a habit of meeting with crowds of young people in the evenings, by simple means of sitting in an open window. It was the first floor window over the entrance to the Bishop's Palace, and the meetings soon became a tradition.

After his death in 2005, the Papal Window has become a kind of monument, with the John Paul II portrait put there permanently.

Wisława Szymborska grave, Rakowicki cemetery,
Rakowicka 26 street

The famous Polish poet and a Nobel Prize laureate, Wisława Szymborska lived in Krakow all her life and was always a prominent participant in its artistic and cultural life. Her poetry both sensual and sensible, always ready to notice the small, humorous absurdities of life, it was much different from the usual patriotic and devout approach most Polish poets had and her poems have achieved critical acclaim and widespread success all over the world, translated into numerous languages including Arabic, Hebrew, Japanese or Chinese.
Following her death in 2012, she was entombed in the family mausoleum on Rakowicki Cemetery.

Piotr Skrzynecki monument
Vis – a – vis coffee house, Main Square 29

Piotr Skrzynecki was a famous director of "Piwnica pod Baranami" cabaret, which has raised the whole generations of polish artists. Piwnica pod Baranami has been the most important fixture of intellectual life of Poland in the post-war communist era. Regarded commonly as a bohemian legend, after his death Skrzynecki was honored with a monument, showing himself sitting at a table in his favorite coffee house "Vis-à-vis", which is still active today.

Czesław Miłosz grave
Skałka Roman Catholic Church, Skałeczna 15 street

Czesław Miłosz was a world-famous Polish poet, especially known for his dedicated opposition to the communist regime. He was awarded Nobel Prize in 1980. His grave is located in the famous "Skałka" Roman Catholic Church, the crypt where Poland's most famous writers are traditionally buried.

Krakow symbols

The Wawel Dragon

The Wawel Dragon is a legendary monster believed to have lived in a cave underneath the Wawel Castle, and the object of a popular tale of a victorious shoemaker, who killed the Dragon by outwitting it. The king of the time, seeing that the city is terrorized by the monster, promised the usual arrangement - half of the kingdom and his daughter hand in marriage - to whoever defeats the beast. A brave young shoemaker (some legends say he was a shoemaker's apprentice), knowing he had no chance in an actual fight, had taken a whole sheep and stuffed it with sulphur, then put it at the entrance to the Dragon's cave. The dragon ate the gift, and the sulphur gave it a flaming indigestion. Feeling terrible, the Dragon ran to the Vistula river and drank so much water that it exploded, and everybody lived happy ever after.

Today, a metal sculpture of the Dragon is put where the Dragon's cave was believed to be, to honor the beast that has become a symbol of the city. The Dragon sculpture breathes fire every five minutes, but it is also possible to request a fiery pandemonium of your own, sending an sms with the text "SMOK" (Polish for "dragon") to the 7168 number.

Horse-drawn carriages

A hundred years ago, horse carriages were the main means of transport in Krakow, and were commonly used like now we use a taxi. They were an important factor of Krakow's everyday life, and today they are part of the city's unique atmosphere, the carriage rides being enjoyed by tourists and also locals (especially for special occasions like weddings). You will see a lot of beautiful carriages on the Main Square, ready for departure till the late evening. The usual carriage tour includes the whole Main Square and the main streets of the Old Town. The prices range from 40 $ / 30 € per hour. The whole carriage is for your disposal, so this cost stays the same up to four persons.

Krakow pretzel

Krakow pretzel is a special kind of hard baked dough snack, sold in three main versions: with salt, with sesame and with poppy seed. Pretzels are very popular in the city and are sold from the special trolleys which can be easily found in the Old Town. The Krakow Pretzel is now officially on the list of Polish Traditional Products approved by the European Union, and is very tasty and cheap (it costs about 0,5 $ / 0,3 €), so make sure you will try one while enjoying our beautiful city.

Map of Krakow center

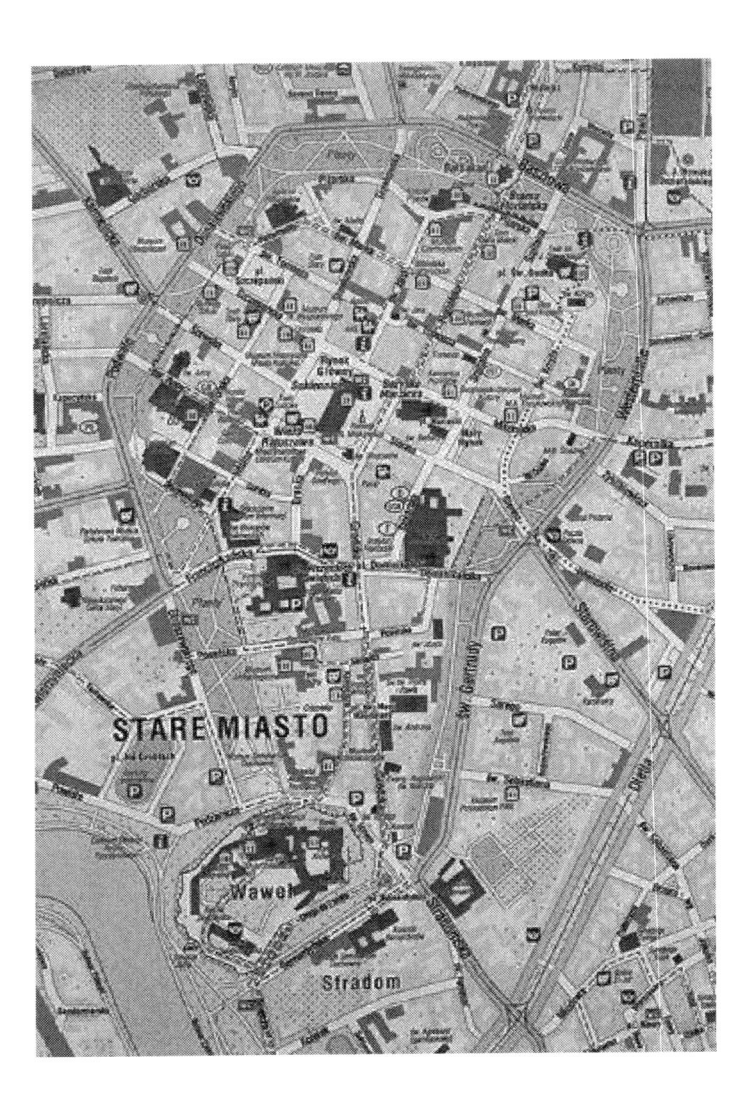

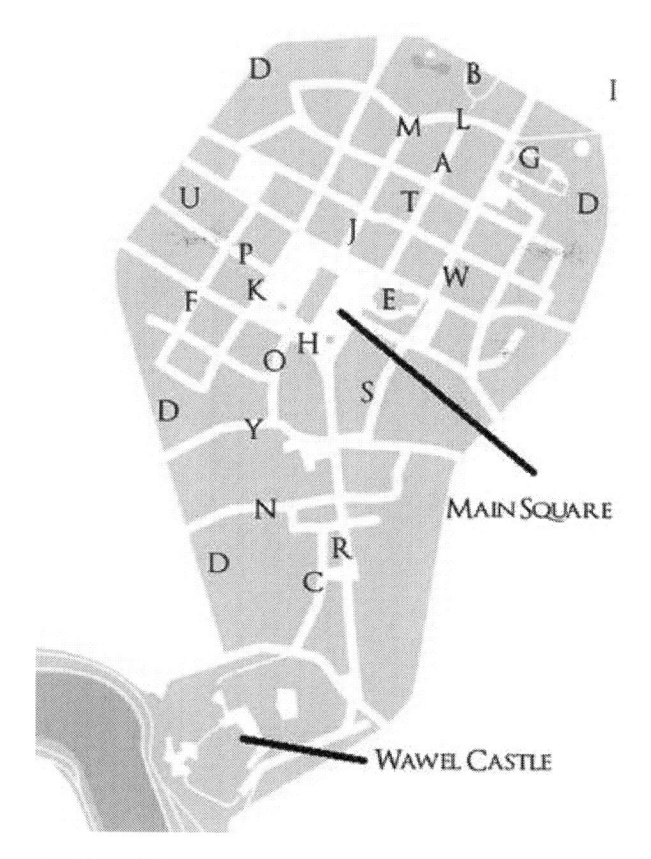

A – Floriańska street

B – The Barbican

C - Kanonicza street

D – Planty park

E – St Mary's Basilica

F – Jagiellonian University Collegium Maius

G – Juliusz Słowacki Theatre

H- Wierzynek restaurant

I – The Main Train station

J - Tourist information center

K - The police station on Main Square

L - St Florian's Gate

M - Czartoryski Museum

N - Archeological Museum

O - Mama's hostel

P - Frantic Club

R - Senacki hotel

S - Pimiento restaurant

T - Pauza Club

U - Bunkier Sztuki cafe

W - Ministerstwo Club

Y - The Papal Window

Copyright 2012 by Adam Kisiel and Agnieszka Kisiel

Photos by Adam Kisiel and Agnieszka Kisiel

adkisiel@gmail.com

Photos of Balice airport, Steel Mill sign, Dumplings, Jan Nowak Jezioranski square, Dachshund dog, Museum of Contemporary Art, Centre map, Trabant car and Wieliczka salt mine licensed by Wikipedia, under the Creative Commons licence.

Printed in Great Britain
by Amazon